THE CORDELL GUIDE TO

STARTING A LANDSCAPE BUSINESS

This is the first in the series of my Cordell Guide Books.


The goal of these books, is to present real life, and a real experiences as well as

to help educate and provide you with a unique experience.

With a simple common sense, realistic approach.

I have worked in many fields in my life and mastered many things.

I am taking my experiences and providing these life events and sharing them with you.

I dedicate this book, to Kimberly and Bonnie, who worked tirelessly in the infancy of my business and helped make it a great success.

**Chapters :**

1.  Getting Started What's In a Name ? pg. 7

2.  Do I Need A License ? pg.11

3.  Company and Needs. pg.13

4.  Covering Your Liability. pg.17

5.  Getting Your First Customer.  pg.19

6.  Billing And Financial Organizing. pg.24

7.  Customers.  pg. 28

8.  Employees. pg. 31

9.  Managing Employees. pg.31

10. The Winter Games. pg.42

11. Problem Solving. pg.48

12. Tips and Tricks of the Trade. pg.53

13. Equipment List.

14. My Closing Thoughts. pg63

**Introduction Page :**

This book is introduced to provide a solid base, for beginning the lawn care or landscape business. This book will contain instructions, as well as tips. The book is designed to not simply tell you how I ran my business in landscaping, but it is designed to give a solid structure to someone looking to start this type of business. There are literally thousands upon thousands of lawn care and landscape companies in the U.S., and it would be a guess that the average city probably contains anywhere from, 10 to several hundred of these types of companies. So this book should help clear the smoke, and give the business owner a good starting point.

There are the two types of major companies that exist, somebody that wants to follow all the rules pay their taxes and make a decent wage. And then exists those that simply throw a lawn mower in the back of their truck and say they are a landscaper or a lawn maintenance company.

This book will show you how one can have a successful business and be taken seriously even mowing lawns, if that's what you choose to do. Many people enjoy simply mowing lawns, plating plants, and perhaps weed control, And if that's all they ever want that's perfectly fine. This book also will help those with other desires to begin the path to a landscape business themselves, because the structure is the same, the tips and tricks of these trades are very similar as you will see in my book.

So finally, there is a book written for the blue-collar business owner. There are many other books to help the blue-collar worker. But only one that helps you run a business and that is this book. As over the years we have been involved in many different types of businesses. Our number one business has been the landscape business. So we are sharing our decades of experience, creating a business, and succeeding in the landscape profession, but have been involved laws, and consulting as well.

So please enjoy this book, and read it thoroughly as there should be something for everyone in here that is wanting a career in servicing outside properties.

**Pre-Thoughts**

So, you decided to open a landscape or lawn care business? From here the decisions to open such a business can be very diverse. In my case at age 12, I went about the neighborhood mowing lawns for about 1.50 per lawn. Now that may not sound like a lot of money but at that particular time as a kid, the minimum wage was 2.25 per hour. So we were making pretty good money as it was very close to what the minimum wage was at the time, me and my friend would manage to make a couple hundred dollars each summer. What I did not know is I was learning to manage, even at age 12.

Why you particularly chose to be in the landscape or lawn care business matters a lot. As most people do not realize it's not simply pushing a lawn mower or emptying trash cans in the back your truck, or hauling them away to the dump's. It takes a lot of planning and coordinating to be successful in a business. Perhaps you worked on your own properties as a child, as I did, maybe you worked after school for a lawn care business or just simply have seen people pushing their lawnmowers around, and thought it's something you would want do?

The fact you decided to make a choice doing it is the first step, so are you looking for a small business to supplement a minimal income? Or perhaps you want to be running a multimillion dollar business? You'll be surprised that both these approaches to a business are the similar. It doesn't matter if you want to be the largest business in the state or simply want to work in your town and make some side money, it's all going to be started the same way and it's going to have some of the same obstacles

This book will contain over 30 years worth of landscaping and lawn care experience. In my past not only was I a successful business owner of the landscape company, I also have studied law and worked in business consulting for several years. So I decided, I would share my many years of experience with the public and help those that want a start such a business headed in the right direction.

So before we begin, ask yourself a couple of questions. Do you mind hard work? Do you mind long hours? Do you mind extreme heats and extreme cold? If your answer to this is no to all three than you are prepared to enter into such a business. It's very important to understand that you will be working out in the elements, and filling a need that businesses and homeowners simply do not want to do themselves, and are hiring out to have it done.

That means it will be in the most undesirable weather at times. The good news is within the first year or two you get used to the changes in the weather. In fact you'll start to enjoy the varied weather that's is out there. (Depending where you live obviously you may have longer winters or summers. )

# Name Chapter 1:  Getting to Started: What's In a Name?

So the first thing to do once you have decided that you want to start a business, is decide the brand or name of your company. Many businesses have grown or failed all based on the names they chose for a business. This may not seem like a major issue, you may want to decide on a name that is spunky or has some pizzazz to it. And why this does have its merits, for a company where your customers are looking for serious work to be done, well they may or may not choose your company if it appears it is more fun, than business.

If you are opening a restaurant or ice cream parlor  well maybe a creative name with a lot of Pizzaz, might be the choice. However if you want to compete in the business world, it will most likely require a very strong business presence to be successful.

When thinking of a name to choose, it is very important to keep this in mind, this being one must imagine from the customers point of view what you look like. What this means is your potential customers  only looking for the job to be completed? Or are they looking for a strong representation of their property.  How you dress, the vehicle you drive, and how your employees conduct themselves on the property will matter a lot. When people hire a service, they want their neighbors or coworkers to be aware that they're hiring a professional to take care of the property they need serviced. So when referring to a name of the business,  it's important to think of the names you may choose. As an example a name like: Get Of Your Lawn, why a catchy name. it may not be something others want in front of their homes in big bold letters.  People are more often to hire something simple like Tony's Lawn Care, why it's not as catchy its direct, now there are problems with something like Tony's lawn care, as it may limit the expansion of that company. Again we are speaking of the creation of the company where the ideal understanding of what the name will do, and what is the ranges of the company's growth expectations, as well as how you want to be seen by the general public that will hire you, is hugely important.

TIPS: The general public looks at key language when choosing a company, oftentimes this is very personal to the choice of the individual. Even if its business related to a company they own. Potential customers are looking to have services completed, they all look for certain key phrases.  And based on the name of the company those key words can mean quite a bit.

**Getting Started: What's In a Name Cont**:

So what are these key phrases that are important to see alongside the business name?

1.  Years in business

2.  Licensed and insured

3.  Services they can complete

4.  Quality of work one can expect

5.  Reasonable rates

These are just a few things that are placed along advertisements flyers, or even the side of the vehicles used for the services. Now looking at the name your business? How will it interact with the above key phrases? A name that can represent itself in a professional manner next to those five choices is a good start when picking the name. Obviously the name with a lot of Pizzaz may not look as professional next to these context words. Not to over think this process but it is really important to understand the name you choose will shape and mold the future of the company. You may not realize it at this moment but even the vehicles you choose, and possibly even a uniform some kind to wear, can be reflected positively by the name choose.

Business Name :

Question :

But what if I already have a name that doesn't fit the ideas in this book?

This will depend on the actual time frame you have operated the business under that name, and how long is the list of established clientele you have. There are one of two things a person can do when they already have an established name and their business is looking to change, rename, or add on to the existing name some services.

As an example: Tony's lawn care could easily be changed to Tony's landscape and lawn maintenance. And it can also be a great time to notify current customers that you're adding fresh and brand new services. Oftentimes, clients become very interested when they see a company they use expanding, it's important at this time as well to ensure the customer knows their services will improve, since you now offer these new services. It is a common feeling all customers have when they hear the company's expanding, they feel that the relationship they had with that business may change. So it is crucial if you are changing your name or expanding to notify your customers personally, and put their minds at ease. That not only will their services be well maintained with these new changes, the abilities to do service for them, will only improve.

TIPS: We will discuss how this can be done in our contracts and billing section in this book.

So to conclude on a business name, keep it simple is the best possible advice one can give you on a name for your business. The bottom line is the more consistent the business name is with the work being completed, the more of a connection the business name will be seen by the public.

TIPS: #1

1. Make sure you allow future growth within the business name chosen.

2. Make sure your name can be connected with future services.

3. Make sure your name reflects a professional atmosphere for professional businesses.

4. Pick a name that allow others to see you as a serious contender in the business world.

TIPS: #2

5. Look for common names not used, oftentimes locality such as city county or state associations are open for your business name. It's also is something that is often overlooked keep that in mind.

6. Keep Pizzaz at a minimum, the more your name contains fluff the more potential customers may see you as less of the serious business, or may not understand your services fully.

7. Keep the length of the name as short as possible, yet allow you to communicate what your business represents.

# What's in a name ?

So let's assume that at this point you have decided a proper name for your business, that's awesome and was the first step to getting your business off the ground.

But there's a little bit more to think about that we must add, this is the legal use of your name, why this is not legal advice it is important that you understand the complexities of even simply naming the business.

Depending on where you live and the laws that apply you may not be able to have a name similar to somebody else's in that city or county you live in. In fact some state laws may limit how your name is listed. Why the majority of states in this country allow open creativity, some local areas put limitations on how a name can be used. There may also be a copyright or trademark on the name you've chosen. Generally speaking if your personal name, such as Tony's landscape business is used, and your name is Tony? This should be fine in most cases. However if your business is named 10 keys landscaping and lawn maintenance(t)(c) and that an name is used or trademarked there could be a problem. Luckily there should be two areas of resources in your state, and the Federal government web sites, where you can check the name for , TM and copyrights. Furthermore you can check your states offices by usually doing an Internet search on their business registry, should pull up the proper information. The list is too vast for information like this to be covered in a book, simple because it can vary from county to county and from state to state.

**TIPS**: Please keep in mind the use of the word "landscape" in your business, may or may not be allowed, depending on where you live. You may only be allowed to call your company a lawn maintenance company. This information should be able to be found in your contractors or state Landscape contractors.

## Chapter 2:  Do  I need to be licensed?

This is probably the most complex question that a person starting a landscape or lawn care business can ask.  This is simply because it varies so much that there's no simple answer one can give, to explain that they need to be licensed, and here's why.

States, counties, cities and even developed monitoring boards such as contractors or landscape boards, may exist and have guidelines of who and what type of business needs to be licensed.  And the licensing varies on what type is acceptable. So let's go over a couple of those.

1.  A contractor's license.  A contractor's license generally requires one or more of the following.  A test or educational process that has granted the contractor certain abilities in their business.  This can vary from plumbing to mechanical to landscaping and everything in between.
2.  A state business license.  This type of license allows the business to operate in the state, it does not grant certain abilities to that existing business.  Generally a state business license only grants the applicant the ability to operate a business.  (We will cover more of this in license and insurance chapter).
3.  Local county and city licenses.  These generally do not allow the applicant certain abilities, and it only allows them to operate a business according to the conditions set by the county.

These are just the most common types of licenses that exist, the contractor's license can be the landscape contractor's license or in some areas lawn maintenance, may require a state license under the contractors classification to operate, again this varies from state to state.

So do you need to have a license to operate?  Generally speaking any business will require some degree of licensing, so it would be expected that if you are opening a legitimate lawn care business there will be the need for a certain kind of license certification of some kind.

You will need in almost all cases, a business license and possibly a state registration license to open a bank account under your business name, or to have operators and liability insurance on the business.

TIPS: In many states acquiring a particular license may not be necessary, but may be desired by your customers.  Nothing says you're a legitimate landscape and lawn care business than having on your fliers, the phone book, or the Internet that you are licensed and insured words placed next to your name.

So even if you are not required to have a license or even insurance, it helps build confidence when people look to hire you, to know that you your equipment, your employees and yourself are covered. In all the years that I operated, I never once had to use my insurance to cover any claims, as it is rare that something happens. But if it does being insured will help.

Tips: Look carefully when operating a landscape company, as many states required a bond t operate.

# Chapter three : Company Type & Needs

So before you can acquire customers, or advertise or pretty do anything, you have to have the ability to finish the work that your hired for. This will probably be one of the longer chapters in my book because it's most likely one of the most important. Many of you may think, hey I got it covered and will skip over this part of the chapter. In fact outside getting paid, this is the number one piece of information needed, so if you read anything in this book you should read this.

You may have worked for a landscaper, or perhaps mowed a few lawns locally. This really doesn't matter allot what drove you to start a business. But the direction you take in the purchase of your equipment can have long-term positive or negative effects on the growth of your company. For the purpose of this chapter we will split this into three categories the landscaper, the lawn care company or someone that operates full landscape maintenance with their business.

## The Landscaper:

OK in the public's eye, the landscaper is somebody that creates large projects in new or existing properties. This can be something from installing sod in a front yard, to designing a whole projects for a new home that's being built. Like ponds, walkways and even decks. The amount of the equipment that can be needed has to be justified for the project. In other words are you going to purchase the equipment needed or find a way to lease or Rent this equipment? As it could be costly. Let's take something simple that generally a contractor would do if they were a Landscaper, a customer calls you and wants a bid on a brand new sod lawn in their front yard, as well as some new plants, plus install a sprinkler system. Right away the amount of Equipment needed is going to vary. To install a sod lawn will require having the sprinkler system installed prior, so obviously the size of this lawn area is going to matter greatly. So will you use a trencher to dig for the pipe, or use physical labor? But the cost of that trencher even rented can be expensive, anywhere from $100 and up per day depending on the size of the project and where you live. Right away you've already effected the amount of profit by having to rent the equipment. Installing and repairing a sprinkler systems in many areas requires a landscape contractor's license, this again will vary from state to state and locality, but generally it does requires licensing to be installed.

Even if there's not a requirement, the materials needed and laying the pipe out, eats into the amount of money needed, so now we have the trencher, pipe, possible a timer. And now have began to install a backflow system (depending on where you live). Plus one must add the amount of man hours it takes to do this, depending on how you approach it. Landscapers generally pick one or two options when it comes to a job they either rent the equipment, or purchase the equipment. If the equipment is purchased, this purchase should always be considered in future jobs. In other words if a piece of equipment cost you $500 you should be looking at trying to cover the cost over the next several jobs when you bid. Generally speaking 17% of your equipment costs in purchasing should be added to the job you're bidding on. This is called applicable purchasing. This allows you over the next several jobs to help pay for the equipment, prior to needing maintenance in most cases. Obviously jobs will vary, and the amount of work needed to complete these jobs, that will vary as well. It would be impossible to write a book and explain every possible scenario, but it is also important to make sure you cover your costs as it will catch up to you at the worst possible time if you don't. ( trust me I know )

If the equipment is rented, this cost should be 100% in the bid for the job. It is important to make sure when you complete any job with rental equipment, that you account for overhead. You may want to add rental cost into future jobs and get a lower bid, but this a ill advised, as generally speaking looking to the future to pay for a cost of rental today does not work. It is best to find a way to cover the rental cost as soon as possible and when renting it should be always on the same job.

**The Lawn care specialist**,

This can be anybody that basically throws a lawn mower in a  truck, and goes about mowing lawns, edging, and blowing off the area when they leave. This is also known as Mow-Blow & Goes. It good honest work, so don't sell it short. But should be also be run legally with all required licenses.

So the question is what are we looking for as far as equipment for the Lawn care specialist?  Well obviously you'll need a lawn mower and a weed eater that can be used as an edger.(these have traversed carburetors meaning they can be turned upside down and still run making the ideal edger, at the fraction of the cost of a horizontal edger ) The other piece of equipment would be a blower these can be either hand held, or backpack depending on the size of your company.  So there three pieces of equipment generally used for a lawn care specialist.  Now, this is very important at this point to realize those three pieces of equipment have the potential use, way beyond how they may built for.  One of the most common things you will find in this type of company will be those who start out with used equipment, possibly their own they had around the home, or the box store purchases of the equipment which is generally affordable to most people but could have questionable durability.

Purchasing those three pieces of equipment can generally be done for around $600 or less, hardly a large business investment, but it will take several lawns being mowed to pay for the equipment that is purchased. (Avoid electric starts, or front driven mowers as they will require more maintenance and have plastic front gears that gum up )

**Landscape maintenance company**, this particular company seems to find its niche in between a full blown a landscape company and a lawn care specialist. These companies generally can be found taking care of lawns, properties, plants and a variety of onetime jobs items such as pruning hedges, planting plants, (that are allowed under your licensing if required). It may even include setting sprinkler timers and light maintenance on those if allowed, and yard cleanups. Generally the lawn maintenance company can care for an entire yard. Not just the lawns themselves, but they are limited to what types of material can be installed legally on the property, as this will vary from state to state and locality, on what's allowed.

The amount of equipment to start a business can be quite costly as a generally require the trailer involved in carrying the equipment needed, as well as many small items.

So we've covered three areas of general services that are provided, the number piece of equipment varies on the vehicle you will use. Next, this has to be the second most important thing listed, is how your vehicle looks when pulling up to a piece of property, as it truly defines how the public sees you. Even at a new landscape construction site, where no one lives, it is important to keep a professional appearance. I cannot tell you how many times I was on job sites and passersby would stop because of the top notch equipment we had, and how clean our vehicles were kept. Also in our area we were the very first company to have a uniform used when conducting services. This set us out among the rest, and to this day local companies do not take the care that we had, in giving a presence of professionalism. But when you are looking at the vehicle you will use, it should be kept neat and clean as possible. This is not mean you need to go out and buy a brand new truck for $40,000? It means your vehicle should look professional. Even a older truck can add a nice look, I did bids in a 67 Ford Truck that was spotless and was a great conversation starter at a estimate.

TIP: Some things, as simple as how much you paid for your truck can mean an awful lot to the customers you have as well as future customers. And here's why, if you are running a business simply mowing lawns, then using a truck that is if the average condition may be more acceptable to the customer because they are looking at how much money you have spent, and the amount of service they are getting cost wise. In other words if you have an average truck, and are charging the prices you are. Will they seem fair to somebody, since the job you are performing is on the lower end of those businesses services, so they understand you may not have the most top of the line truck and equipment, if you're simply mowing lawns.  However if you are the landscape company or a landscape maintenance company then that condition of that vehicle and the age of the vehicle may matter to the customer. The geographic locality plays a part as well.

# Chapter Four : Covering Your Liability.

We're just about ready to start business, but there's one thing we need to make sure we're covered for the work that were doing, in case there's an accident. This does not mean just on the job, it means if you own a vehicle and are using it for work purposes in a legitimate business, you will have to have proper insurance for the job you're doing. So let's go over a couple of things here, and present you a list of things to consider when looking at insurance and liability coverage.

1. You may choose not to cover your vehicle for business, as it's one you use at home and to mow lawns. This may seem like a good idea? However if you place signs on the side of your truck advertising yourself as a business, and are any accidents? Chances are your insurance company will not cover the damages to your vehicle, or worse may cancel your insurance. It is not that much more to pay for insurance on your vehicle, But as a business, it's important to do so.
2. If you own the landscape company or a landscape maintenance company depending on the state you live in you may be required to have licensed and bonding prior to starting your company. Some contractor boards will require this.
3. If you have someone working for you other than a family member and you're running a legitimate business it will be up to you to provide proper coverage for your employees.
4. Now regardless of the business you open even if it's a lawn mowing business you will want to have some form of liability insurance while you are performing your duties on somebody else's property. Their homeowner's insurance will not cover you on their property in most cases, unless they were negligent as a property owner. See your state and local laws to be sure. In any event say you are mowing the lawn and the mower shoots out rock and it hits your customer's car? What will you do? The vehicle may cost more than the income you're getting from the customer. Even worse if the rock happens to unfortunately hit a individual you, have a major problems on your hands if you have no insurance.
5. Insure the trailer as well as its contents, you have to ask the insurance company as in most cases, the vehicles insurance may not cover it.

The idea of covering yourself for the liability of your duties on the job matter, it also helps not having to worry about an accident that may happen. The landscape company can have a very high insurance cost, and liability costs, so be sure to check.

Generally speaking lawn mowing and landscape maintenance companies can find a much lower cost of insurance due to their light foot print on properties.

TIP: many cities and counties will not allow you to have a business license in their jurisdiction, if you do not have the proper insurance, again this will vary from town to town and from county to county. So it's very important to be aware of the insurance requirements of the areas you will do business in.

The above information is not legal advice, as I cannot provide that for you, it is a guideline of general specifications what may be required depending on where you live. Please make sure before you take on one customer that you have the proper coverage to protect your business and employees.

Special Notes:

While this information may seem very short and to the point, there are some other aspects to keep in mind :

Your insurance company may require you to list the cities or counties you will do business in, furthermore the insurance company may place limitations on the type of work they will cover. For an example, if you were to begin planting plants in your landscape maintenance business and had not done this before, your insurance company may not cover you for ( pipes etc) because of the possibility of water lines, gas lines, and different utilities that could be harmed by your actions. Not only this, but depending on the city you live in, you may only be able to dig down so many inches before you are required to have the area marked by the city or county and require as well as extra insurance coverage. I know this sounds extreme but depending on the state, county, they may have set up some very strict guidelines for even planting plants. So before you head onto your first job or contract, it is crucial to have the proper insurance should you need to protect yourself.

# Chapter 5  Getting Your First Customer

Well, we now have everything in place to get our first customer, we've accomplished all of the goals we needed to this point to get a new customer.  You may be reading this book because you are looking to advance to new projects, or to upgrade the services you currently do?  However this chapter will apply to anybody if they're looking to enhance what they have, or start off new, this chapter will help you.  After decades of research and testing this is some of the best information I can provide.  Please keep in mind when reading this information, we're providing this from thousands of hours, and thousands of customers, so this is the information that we're giving, based on what was the best way to accomplish the goals we needed. Demographics and Geographic locations, will be the key element to how you will get your first customer.  It will be crucial to know the customer base that's out there, meaning things like groups, clubs, organizations and even if you exist near a military base, all these things  have impact on how you gather your first customer. ( Note:  understanding area age groups is a plus)

You may already see this, and think you will just give senior discounts and that's all you need to know about this chapter?  That would be incorrect, as this chapters answers questions of how to get your first customer.  The problem is if you give a discount to one customer that qualifies with the criteria you have set up, that will become a standard for what other future customers get and may be shared by word of mouth.  So it's not simply giving a 10% or 15% discount.  Its understanding the growth with that discount .  So let's look at it this way you end up going into a neighborhood and are hired for mowing the lawn four times a month and you're going to charge $50.00 a week.  Minus that 10% discount.  If you have several customers in a neighborhood that you applied this discount you can be looking at as much as several $100 in discounts in the same area, so this can add up quickly.

In the neighborhoods that we had our business there was specific areas where we found a concentration of seniors, moreover there were areas that we found a little bit higher concentration of Veterans.  However this was learned by trial and erro at the time we had started, we were unaware of demographics even being part of the businesses, as we were looking at the yards themselves and not the clients.  That is the key elements to get your first customer, is understanding who they are, not just the property they own.  As well as how you will adapt these expenses and discounts. I am not saying avoid giving discounts.  In fact our greatest accomplishments and understanding our customer base, was in giving discounts accordingly.  It is amazing how $5.00 a week off of a client's service charges makes a difference on how they feel about paying out the funds each month.

TIPS: We found out that we secured more long-term customers by giving out a discount in the beginning. We also found the same customers would look to us for one-time services such as hedge trimming, yards cleanups and landscape projects.

Note: It is important to not modify the discount to adjust for the services you are providing. If you are going to give a discount? Then you must give a honest discount. Do not raise the bid of a service, only to discounted the percentage. Why the customer may not be aware that you've done this, starting off the agreement with your customers with a lie is the wrong way to do business.

Logistics, just like the demographics, are key elements to the affordability of a business.

Example: A customer has called, and needs a bid on a lawn care job approximately 10 miles from your location. This area is well within the service areas you would normally do a service. And it takes you approximately 20 minutes to the job site. If you have a crew you will be paying that crew for that 20 minute drive to the job site, and back from the job. That is a combined time for the employee of 40 minutes each sitting in the truck. (if you have an employee.) This is also 40 minutes of downtime not earning income. This all has to be included in the jobs you bid, so be sure to include traveling distances. Let's imagine this is the only customer you have 10 miles away, and you only have a handful of customers. And are just taking just about anyone that calls right now to hire you. You do this to get your business off the ground. But! You must be able to justify having a customer that requires travel time.(Travel time would be seen as anything taking more than 5 to 10 minutes to the next job). So you've agreed to a contract 10 miles from your home, or shop, and you rarely get another client out in area? This is where the problem can be costly, if not bid properly to include travel time or down time, it has the real ability to eat into profits very quickly. So when you are bidding with longer distances keep in mind that cost to get there and back in the bid. You can always go back to your customer and let them know ( once you have now gathered many more customers) You are now going to give them a discount. ( Because you are spending more time in that location), You can always word that the way you'd like, but it really will impress the customer that's been a loyal customers in the area, that they are now are getting a discount because of it.

Logistics, also involved is the amount of fuel you use any given day for the jobs you are performing. Some will take a riding lawn mower to use on a property, that they can finish in about 30 minutes. It is important to keep in mind that the larger equipment will use more fuel and there's more wear and tear on the vehicles, as well is the possibility to incur expenses or breakdowns greater.

All these things have to be kept in mind when you're bidding on the job, as well as even how long it takes you do it, and how long it is to the next job. Another key issue to think about is how long it takes you to set up and break down on your job. It's not simply doing the services, it is also having the vehicle and equipment ready for the next job that's why looking for customers within 5 to 10 minutes from each other or less is the ideal situation. Why this may not be something you can accomplish in the very beginning it is very important to try and concentrate in those areas, and use this as a business goal and model.

**Getting your first customer continued: Getting the word out.**

So we now know where, and how you will be seeking your next jobs, so the next logical steps are getting the word out.

The biggest mistake that I save seen businesses do when starting out, is spending an excessive amount of their funds in advertising. You'll hear from others, that advertising is one of the largest parts of their business expenses. This is true, however the method used has to yield the maximum return, this means TV ads and the radio as examples are not great resources for new businesses, and those looking to expand. It has been found that the cost for a commercial using TV & Radio, far exceeds the amount of time a more simple method can be used to reflect the better use of funds. Fact is the most effective form of advertising, is also the most economical. This is because it involves generating a large map area using fliers. An average fliers, (depending on who does the printing) should run between 2 to 3¢ ea. It is also advised to get several 1000 copies of your flyer. This is because most large box stores and copy services tend to give the best price, when you have 1000 copies or more, so be prepared to spend a little bit of money to get these copies the first time.

It is crucial as you design your first flier to not designed one as to where it can only be active for a limited time. You may end up with many fliers that you cannot use if you do not allow them to be multipurposed. Your very first flier should not contain a lot of junk. Have you ever been driving down the street and taken a look at a yard sale sign? They will try and place directions the date and the address all into little piece of paper that you're traveling by at 35 miles an hour. That form of advertisement is wasted, as the person passing by knows it means something is for sale, but they don't know what. So now they're going to have to figure out what that signs said for that yard sale. Now why this is an applicable to landscaping? Is you have 3 to 5 seconds with a flier to get that customer's attention once they've seen it. The more detailed, and the longer the information is, the less people will take notice.. The internet blankets short, concise advertising, and so have I also implemented the same form of advertising into simple flyers. Fliers can be used at a fraction of TV and Radio ads and allow target advertising.

This is why we are against using TV and radio ads for a landscape businesses, as one can do better with a little bit of leg work.

TIPS: On flier placement.

1. Do not place flyers inside or on a mailbox this is illegal to do so.
2. Do not place flyers in newspapers that may be left on a doorstep or in a box.
3. Do not leave fliers on homes that say no soliciting.
4. Do not leave fliers on vehicles in parking lots, the property owners may ban you from future access.
5. Place a flier on the outside of the door or storm door /screen door. Do not open any doors, or gates.
6. You may want to place a flier at the edge of a doormat this may keep it from flying away.
7. The best time to place fliers is on the weekends, as you're more apt to run into a potential customer this way, and have a discussion, as opposed to leaving a flier.

**Getting the word out continued: contents of a flier.**

This is where you finally get have some fun, you want a professional looking flier, something that catches the eye of the customer, and something simple yet Identifiable like a lawn mower or a picture of a tree with hedges near it. The important part is any graphics you put must reflect your business services. It should be subtle and about 1/8 of the size of the flier, and generally it should be centralized, logos are great if you have one. At the very top, you can use fancy fonts to show your business name, however standard fonts should be used for easy reading in the rest of the flier. At the top along with a business name, you should have the city and phone number. Nothing else should be there as it gets crowded and makes it hard to see. You'll want to include an e-mail that at the bottom of the flier, not the top, as the idea is you want the customer to read the entire flyer and notice there's information at the bottom that is the best way to place advertisements on a flier.

Have you ever heard the expression keep it simple stupid? So I'm not suggesting your customers or yourself are stupid, but you really want the flier plain and simple. The rest of this flier should only have limited information such as.

- Reasonable rates
- Senior discounts
- Veterans discount
- Locally owned and operated(yes people assume that, but for some reason saying it makes them think).
- The top five services you do, or weekly services, lawn mowing and landscape maintenance, sprinkler repair, Sod and landscaping, etc.

And that's about all you should put on a flier, there may come a time during the year you may want to run specials such as fall leaf cleanup, spring cleanups, holiday specials, these type of things you can do, depending on how much time you have to do it.

TIPS: A personal note, it takes an awful lot of time and dedication to start a business of any kind.  However it is just as important to understand that your family and friends are just as important to you, and actually will serve as a backbone to your business.  So why being dedicated your business really benefits it, you must stay grounded with family or friends, as well as groups you may belong to, all help keep you grounded.

Notes:

This can also be a great time if you chose to get business cards to include those in your existing customer's newsletters, giving your customers a couple of extra cards can allow them to pass along to friends and family.  Also for customer specific business cards, you can also get those with a magnetic backing, which allows the customer to put it on the refrigerator for easy access.

## Chapter 6: Billing and Financial Organizing:

How you decide to collect money is basically what we're addressing, there can be many ways you may choose to be paid. You have several options:

- Leave a billing statement in their door.
- Send a statement in the mail.
- Leave a receipt for a cash payment.

Let's go over a couple these first.

If you plan on leaving a billing statement in their door, and if you're clients are on a weekly service and they paid either for that month or if they prepay for services? By leaving a statement in the door two weeks prior to the next billing cycle will be the most economical way to do so. However, the problem with leaving a bill in the door, is you never know for sure the client got your statement. We had done this for quite awhile, and over time, more clients would state they never got a bill. Tried things like putting them in the crack of the door, so when the door opened the bill would be there. Many things we tried, but about one out of 10 clients would say they did not get the bill. Now we have no way of knowing if that was true or not. The problem with that situation is you will have to address it by contacting the customer, and saying you were not paid. That automatically places an aggressive view of situation to your customer, especially if the client truly did not get the statement, and has no idea what you're talking about. So leaving a statement on the door, is the most economical way of doing it, but also it does have its flaws. Sending a statement in the mail, why this may not be the most cost effective with an average cost per customer of light around 50¢, this can easily add up to the costs. However if done properly you can easily cover that 50¢ with the added on services.     And below......... this is how it's done!

Newsletters with billing . The first thing you do is create a newsletter not a flier, letting them know that at particular times a year, there are services you could do that are above and beyond their normal contract they have with you. I cannot tell you how many hundreds of jobs, if not thousands, we got by simply letting people know we also had seasonal services we can provide, this could be leaf cleanup, dethatching, winter sprinkler system draining,  and spring clean up services. But you get the idea, as mentioned in early chapters, knowing the demographics and customer base you have, and using that material you can customize newsletters that will fit a general description of the customers you have. This can also included snow blowing, if it's something you choose to do is a business in clearing walkways during winter.

There is literally no end to the amount of services you can add to a newsletter. You can offer special or offer 20% off one month's bill for referrals. Something like this really helps cover the costs of sending through the mail. This also ensures a 99.9% payment rate.  When we switched from billing in the doors, to billing through the mail, we no longer had many late payments, or missing payments, which guaranteed the stability in our business finances.

**Billing and financial organization continued:**

On this particular area we will cover cash payments, which can also mean a check handed to you for one time services.  It is important to carry a small receipt book for those times you are doing single jobs.  Why,  you do want to have a contract with the customer, cash payment should be either noted on the contract or through cash receipts.  This is important if you have other employees collecting funds, as this ensures accurate collection from your clients.  And employees are protected for accusations of theft, or jobs not being completed.(We will go into employees in a later chapter).

It should be noted, all receipts should have the customer's name and address as well as the amount collected, plus a check number on the receipt.  Depending on your customer, they may hire you for Rental Properties, or something along those lines, and having documentation will be important to them.  If you're using a receipt that does not have your business name always keep a business card with you and provide that to the customer at the time you did the service.

## Keep proper books.

It is very important to review contracts and your cash payments,  and make sure keep them documented.  A simple ledger can allow you to place many customers in a page.  There also a computer programs that will help you manage and bill your customers.

Since you own a business, that means you have a tax ID number, which also means you need to be accountable for the funds that are collected.  If you have a client that has hired you to take care of their Rental Property, and they include this information on their taxes when filed, and you are ever audited, you may be contacted to verify the services you provided.  If you have no information you could be in trouble with the IRS and your local tax revenue department.

**Special Note** : I was in the lawn maintenance & Landscape business, and observed many fly by night businesses that deal strictly in cash and personal checks.  Why some businesses operate this way, and keep their business away from tax revenue sources, it is illegal and wrong way to do business.  Most likely if you have chosen to run an illegal business? My book will not apply to you, because this is how to run a legitimate business.  It will mean proper records, proper insurance, proper registration of your business and operations.  You may think that running a business under the table will make it easier.  I can assure you it will make it harder.  If you're a non license business or operating under the table, and are injured, your insurance company may not cover you, if your vehicle is an accident while operating a business under the table your vehicle may not be covered.  Services may be rendered for a client that refuses to pay, no collections company will take you serious if you've advertised as a business, and ran that business under the table and not on the books.

 This is why you'll find in my books I am 100% against cash flow only, when run as a under the table businesses, as they are not legitimate, and confuse the public about costs and other things.  A fly by night business with no overhead for taxes and running costs that are required, can underbid the the average legitimate company.  This is unfair and illegal, so please run your business as it should be run, legally.

**Taxes:**

Due to the overwhelming tax system in this country, it would be impossible to cover all areas of business and the tax system.  Why this is not legal advice, I will be giving some general information we are aware of at the time this book is published,  please take it upon yourself to verify anything you read in this book when it comes legality and taxes.

The tax system while running a business may require you to pay taxes at the Federal, state, county, and even some city levels.  Many areas of the tax system will require you keep in itemized list of your equipment, and stocked on hand.  For example you may carry 20 extra bags of fertilizer or seed, this needs to be documented when you file taxes in some instances.  So it is very important as noted, keep solid records of what you buy, and what you spend.  If you use a proper ledger that allows a check numbers to be input, this will serve all the better for records.  The more you keep information in the same area the easier it can be accessed when it's needed.


The good news is that any person starting out a legitimate new business can often use the startup costs and equipment as deductions when filing their taxes.  In fact some areas may even give tax incentives to new businesses in the area.  Your chamber of commerce, or local City Hall and county offices can give you a better direction.

I apologize but there are literally millions of cities in the United States and it would be impossible to advise anybody on the accuracy of the tax system in your area.

Tax is something we don't want to pay, we want to avoid at all costs it's just how we feel about it.  But the majority of new and small businesses get in hot water when they have not done their due diligence to find out how their business needs to be operated.  It would be advised when you're starting out your business to contact a tax specialist to get advice on the proper way to keep records.  Please do not take this lightly, as it is common knowledge to those in the business world, that taxes not properly kept can undermine the operations of business and force a closure.  However if you do things properly you will not even notice that you paid taxes, or had to file taxes because you did the retain records the right way.

**TIP:** keep in mind when doing a bid on a job to include a percentage of that profit that will require taxes to be paid on it.  This is why contacting a tax specialist so they can advise you on your potential income and what tax bracket you will be in.  For example if you have a 10% bracket you'll want to keep in mind of the amount needed as a deduction from the funds you've collected.

I realize writing this book that most people probably will overlook this area of taxes and will figure it's overly complicated and they're not going to worry about it.  To say that taxes are the most important part of a business? Well that that would be false, but it is crucial to be accurate and updated on records to ensure you don't have problems later on.

## Chapter 7: Customers: keeping the ones you have, and attracting new ones.

This is probably the most fun part about the book you are reading, as this is where your own creativity of owning a business, and doing duties for properties can come out. Creativity is something you'll have to do on your own, this next section of the book will give you some ideas on how to figure that out, to be sure which direction to head.

### What customers like.

Generally speaking, customers have hired for one of two reasons, they are not able to do the work they're hiring you for, or they don't want to do the work they're hiring you for. In any case they are wanting a particular job completed that will benefit the exterior landscape of their house or business. It is very important from this point of view, to understand what a customer is looking for. They want reliability, as well as a nice presentation of their home. They also want surrounding businesses or neighbors to see they actually care about where they live or work. Most of those could drive through our cities and easily identify those that care about their homes and those that don't. Generally speaking, it is very easy to simply look at the front yard of the home and get the impression that they don't care. Whether this is accurate doesn't matter, but the homeowner wants to hire you for a purpose, so please keep that in mind.

With the above in mind, this is why it is important that your representation of your company is seen clear when completing services  It is also why I mentioned in other chapters why a nice clean vehicle, and the well dressed employee, gives the impression to the customer they've spent their money wisely, and in turn this show's others that they spent their money wisely.

So how does this get you new customers?  Well, why we are not teaching marketing in this book, this is exactly what you are doing. You are providing a situation to be observed by potential customers, as well is peers of the clients you hire. It is very easy to drive down neighborhoods or business streets and see the people that maintain their properties. This is what is called free advertising, you are doing a job at a specific place and are observed by passersby, who view the work you are doing, and are impressed. Possibly enough to contact that business or neighbor that is a customer of yours. In our many years of work, we found a high percentage of jobs were based on the homes or businesses we are already completing. This is why earlier in this book we have discussed not using radio and TV for this particular type of business, as it does not justify the cost no matter how well the salesperson may try and convince you otherwise TV and radio are not ideal for these types of services.

So let's digress a little bit back to keeping the clients you have.

Doing your job and doing it well, definitely has its perks in keeping a current client, and ensures they are happy with the service to that point. Simply doing the job is not enough, I'm going to throw out a couple of tips to help you identify possible problem areas.

- If you or your employees are smokers never ever smoked on the job even on break if you are located on or near the customers property.
- Ensure you keep the extra change of clothes and try and be as clean and neat as possible when working. Wearing a hat and keeping your shirts buttoned helps gives a professional appearance.
- Do not ever allow your employees to argue among themselves or with you; moreover to not reprimanded a employee ever on a job site, save that for when you're back at your shop.
- Do not allow arguing or reprimanding in your vehicles. Others may see you and this gives a bad image.
- Never ask to use a customer's bathroom facilities unless it's a dire emergency, most customers will see this as an invasion of privacy even though you're on their property.
- Do not ask to use a client's phone. If cost is an issue get a prepaid phone and keep it with you, as those can be had for around 20 to 30 dollars a month.
- Make sure you communicate any problems at once with your customer, or any damage to property. Never cover up a mistake. Be honest and upfront about anything that did not go as planned with your customers. ( As I covered earlier do not lie in your business practices)
- Taking a break at your truck is perfectly fine, even having a small snack. But if at all possible take your lunch break away from the client's property. For some reason clients see this as a form of laziness, even know you're entitled to take a break for lunch.
- Keep your vehicle clean, the outside appearance of your vehicle and equipment matters.
- Notify Customer ASAP when you see unforeseen added costs to a them . They may or may not want the extra cost, so  get approval in writing prior to any services.
- Be on time, unless weather or an emergency prevents this, notify client as soon as possible. As nobody wants to wait to find out you will not be there on time.
- Be consistent with weekly services, it would be helpful for the client to know the exact day you'll be out. Try to accomplish that goal and stick to it.

- Don't surprise clients with hidden fees , like fertilizer or hauling debris away, as many customers may assume some services are included.  So make sure your contract reflects exactly what you'll be doing. Don't assume anything.
- Have fun, be happy and content when on the job, even if you are not is crucial. Body language can be seen by a customer and it reflects on how they feel about you.
- Keep home at home, and keep work related issues at work.!!

# Chapter8: Employees & Partnerships

If you're planning on having a business with more than just yourself doing the services, you will need employees. You'll have to determine how many employees you need at a given time. How you choose to do this can have a lot of impact on your business and its costs.

Starting out you'll have to decide, will you hire a part time employee, a fulltime employee or maybe a temporary employee? Let's go over a couple of those and see what the pros and cons are. There are three types of employees.

**Temporary employees**. This may be the easiest way to get an employee and cover all the needed costs all in one place. Depending on your contract with the temp agency, they will cover your taxes your insurance and payroll to that employee. The temp employee can be someone you choose to work with few days, or indefinitely until the company grows. This is probably a great choice for a lawn maintenance company, or someone that simply mows lawns as a service. The reason being training or finding the kind of experience needed should not be that difficult. Within a very short amount of time, a average person with little or no training can mow a lawns, use a blower and do edging. In fact you can customize your requests to the temp agency, that you would like someone that has some experience with a lawn mower or mowing lawns and light yard work. The only problem with a temp employee is the dedication from that employee can vary. When a person is unsure how long their employment will be, it is very hard to get the kind of dedication you may want. This is very different from what you would get from a fulltime hired employee. Also depending on your agreement with your employees, a noncompetitive agreement may be very difficult if not impossible to hold to a temporary agency or employee. Meaning you may train somebody and they quit the temp agency, and start their own lawn care business. Plus they have the potential aspect of going after your clientele. There is the pros and cons to any employee setup.

**Part time employees.** This is probably the most difficult employee to hire as this person will either be on a set amount of days each week or on call. Training an employee that is part time, means they may seek employment elsewhere, because they're not getting the fulltime hours a need from you. They may also pick up another job to compensate their income. Plus in most cases and employee is not going to sign a noncompetitive clause agreement when they're not even on a fulltime basis. You may be able to get by on a fulltime / part time basis depending on the hours that legally defined this in your area. The part time employee will also learn all of the tricks of the trade you know, and also may go after your clients. They may decide to open their own business, this is why the part time and temporary employees are very difficult choices for a new company. But they are the most cost effective.


**Fulltime employee.** In most businesses having a fulltime employee even if it's just one other person allows the stability of your business to grow. It also allows your employee to trust that the company will be around for quite awhile. They see that they hold a key position to its future, if they do a good job for you. Having a fulltime employee really identifies your company as one thats growing, and that you are serious business to contend with. Having a fulltime employee also means your services can be stretched a little bit farther, than one can their self, or part time . You can also implement alongside a fulltime employee a temporary help for larger jobs, or could hire a part time employee to work with you. It should be noted some fulltime and part time employees will require insurance that will vary based on the requirements in the area you live. But generally speaking if you're running a legitimate licensed and insured business it will be required that any employees you have, are covered under specific conditions. Due to the overwhelming information on something like this, it cannot be included in the book because it varies from state to state and locality as well as jurisdictions.

A fulltime employee also has the ability to really benefit your company as it grows, by allowing them to step up to a managing or supervisory role. Oftentimes the supervisors in the fledgling company become the managers when your business has expanded, and they are used to how things run. However having an employee on the payroll whether as part time or fulltime will require accurate tax procedures. It will also require specific pay dates an employee insurance protections. ( Can vary depending on where your business is located). As you can see this becomes a very complicated process in hiring a fulltime employee, or part time employee that will be on the books. It should be noted this changes the dynamics of the business, but its a crucial choice with long lasting effects. So it has to be included in your bids for a new client, on how it will help cover all costs for that employee.

**Partnership.** A partnership can be a great thing or it can destroy your company. There are pros and cons to having a partnership. Most Pros have to do with the elimination of employee benefits and costs. It also allows you to split the cost and responsibilities of running the company with your partner. This also means all the profits are generally split with a partner. If you were starting a company out, and did not have personal insurance on the two partners? It could also greatly effect insurance costs. But It would still require that both of you have proper insurance on the vehicles and liability and bonding as required. The partnership allows two likeminded individuals to split the duties of business. There are very successful partnerships that are out there, in fact our business ran as a partnership from its very beginning and until we closed the business it operated as a partnership.

The pros of a partnership:

Generally speaking. Partnerships in a business, share the same passion and desires for success. They realize or they should realize, performing their duties at peak performance has the potential of making their business a huge success. But is a shared success, no one person controls the outcome of that business and its success. That is why a meeting of the minds. as it's called has to be clear. The benefits of a partnership is that it adds reliability for your customers, and for your operations. If one person is sick or unable to do the job that day, a partner will add to the stability. The number one pro for having a partnership has to be stability.

The cons of a partnership:

As mentioned that meeting of the minds, is crucial for a partnership. Being each and every one of us thinks and acts differently, and may even respond differently in different situations. Well this can cause uneasiness in the business and possible conflicts. It is for that matter that partnerships require a very clear understanding of the duties of each partner. And they should not overlap. Overlapping of duties can add to difficulties. It would be unlike going to a restaurant and having two cooks making your meal. This is not done in the restaurants for the same reason a partnership in the business should not be done. One person does one job, and another person does the other. That's how it's supposed to work. However in a partnership oftentimes you'll find someone knows how to do something better than the other partner, and overtime they will share that information with a partner causing potential issues, prompting a debate.


Partnerships are basically co-owners, and it means your company is responsible for splitting costs, the income, and the liability. It also means if there's a problem with the business it becomes the problem of both of yours. It also means major decisions have to be agreed upon by both parties, unless those responsibilities have been already separated by the partnership agreement. ( have one in writing )

This is why it is highly advised that the two persons that have formed a partnership, are allowed to do duties, and supervise or delegate duties under specific conditions that are pre-approved. As an example one partner manages the income, or all the finances and any taxes. One person sets policies under those duties. The other partner manages the daily operations and logistics of the jobs in the field. By both partners may do the physical work. Only one partner in the field would manage the jobs. This can be difficult and certain aspects of the job, when duties are being delegated. A partner explaining to the other partner, they must all pull weeds, why they the manager of the duties on the site, are going to sit on a riding mower in mow the lawn. Something as simple as those duties can build animosity, so it is very important if you're going to choose a partnership to sit down, and be extremely clear of how the duties are lined up. It's no mystery of partnerships only work if there's a clear understanding of the duties that need to be performed.

# Chapter 9:  Managing the employees :

Myself having been a owner of several businesses, and having worked extensively in management and supervisory roles, so with this knowledge I'm presenting the area of expertise I have.

What is an employee?  An employee is the physical extension of your companies business.  They alone are the backbone of any business.  This also includes, if you're a sole owner and you're the only employee, as the majority of people that will hire you for a product, or services, will see the employee as the extension of that company.  Even the largest companies that exist in the consumer market, are represented solely by the employees that work for them.  Anyone can own the company but not anyone can have good employees.  However having a good employee is 100% the responsibility of those who run the company.  If you've hired a employee that performs poorly that is not  just a reflection of the employee, it is a reflection of your poor managing, in running the company.  After all you gave them the job, you interviewed them, and you alone chose them to be an employee of your company, furthermore you have provided the training and equipment the employee uses.  If you have an employee that does not do the job needed, this is the responsibility of the business owner.  It also means you are responsible for fixing the problem, as the employees are not going to fix the problem themselves, even if you make them aware of it.  That is why this chapter is designed to give the business owner some tools and insight, as to what is occurring when you have employees.  Now I mentioned in the above paragraph, even if you are the sole employee, "Yes" you are also responsible for how your own conduct is. As your sole employee, it is very easy as a business owner to decide what policies you wish to follow.  This should not be a negotiable thing, even if you are the only employee as standards should be set and met by the employees no matter if it's one person or 5000. You are responsible as the owner to make sure the businesses is run properly.  And yes there are landscape maintenance companies that have thousands of employees,  and have even franchised their businesses, so yes there can be many standards that need to be kept, and you are responsible for it.  So now that we've beat that to death we can continue with the rest of the chapter here.

**Hiring an employee,** you will have to set standards of conduct for your company, and you'll also have to set policies for your employees.  Why these can be made up over time they can be confusing to any employees you may hire, if there's not a clear cut explanation of what is expected from them.  It is at this time I would highly suggest you sit down and go from the beginning of the day's work, to the ending, as well as the days - you will pay your employees, and make the list right on down to time off, and how you will deal with showing up late etc.  It would be impossible in this book to cover how to hire a good employee. ( It will be in future managing books Coming out early 2019)

**Managing employees continued:**

With the complexities of employees, and the dynamics involved with them, has become more detailed in the last decades or so. The questions that come up in the political arenas are judging the operations of nearly all businesses. While we're not going to address any the political issues here, there are however political aspects that have been added to the workplace in the last decade. You may be required depending on your state or city's position, have new set guidelines on how these new additions are dealt with. Gender equality, identification, are a small example of sensitivities businesses are now being placed at the threshold of dealing with. This itself can create a offset scenario of rules, you must meet as well as understand those dynamics, as it may change when you're forced to identify these additions, and make changes to the way the businesses is run. This addition to this chapter is simply here to help you be aware and, ask the right questions with in the locality of your business. We will not address this further, as the rest of the chapter will still give you tools to be aware of, and how to deal with them. Remember this is not legal advice but suggestions, it'll be your due diligence to take the information I am providing here, and determine whether it's applicable to your situation where your businesses is. It is simply impossible when it comes down to the legal obligations and the amount of cities, and regulations throughout the state's to write a book that's going to cover everything.

To be the manager you must understand there are clear definitions between being the owner of the business and managing the business . They are not the same, that is why we discussed earlier in partnerships those two specific duties must be separated as the future of the company depends on it. This is also where policies come into play.

Setting policies, it seems as if it would be the easy task, as you know what you want from your company and now you are at the point you have an employee, so in your mind obviously you have what it takes to get clients, and help your business grow. ( Hopefully this book has helped you up to this point). Now we must address employees and policies. Here are several ideas to keep in mind.

- What is your tolerance for the specific policies set?
- What are your resolution practices for specific policies?
- Do your policies spread over into, conduct and interactions with clients?
- Will your policies vary from an employee to employee depending on position?
- Who will enforce the policies?
- Will the manager, owner, or both set policies and enforce them?
- Will there be a review of policies, if they are violated prior to enforcement?
- Will your policies include time off, vacations, arriving late?

These are it for right now, and will vary depending on the size of your business. It is highly advised that you sit down with your business planner or partner and develop policies for your employees. Regardless of the position and its duration policy should be set prior to hiring.. ( See Meltdowns Guide to Managing Businesses , book coming out Spring 2019 )

## Managing employees Part 2:

In this chapter we will manage problem solving, and are assuming you have set policies that reflect the problems finding the solution. Knowing the policy was violated, or not followed, is the first part in approaching a employee about the problems and concerns you have.

When managing a company it is important to address the issues, as your are made aware of them, except on the job site. If on the job, you should wait if possible, and approach the employee as soon as you can, to let them know the concern(s) you have. As noted in earlier chapters, you are on service calls for your clients, you are not there to manage the employees, and enforce policies unless it's absolutely necessary to do it on the job site. What you see is what they see!

Approaching the employee about the problem is the first step. The next step is to have the information you need to enforce and discuss the policy in your possession, that is why it is always a good idea to keep your policies in your glove compartments of your truck or vehicles, that you use in your business.

Employees do not like to hear they have not done a great job, this is more heavily enforced by the employee, when they are tired at the end of the day, it's hot outside, or it's freezing cold outside. A tired employee, is more apt to not pay attention when you are speaking to them, as opposed to when they are rested, and ready for a conversation. This may not be always applicable, but that is the ideal situation. Also it is best if possible to discuss these things at the end of the day not the beginning. Addressing an issue with an employee unless it's crucial, should be avoided until the workday is wrapping up. You want the employee on the job site thinking about the job, not thinking about the policies you just discuss with them, and how you may be displeased with their conduct, or actions regarding a policy.

Of course everyday is different, that's what makes landscaping, lawn care and landscape maintenance fun to do. It also means each day could vary when you'll have the opportune moment speak to your employee. It should be noted the advice that we're giving you should only be when safety or urgency, is not mandatory at that time. If there is a safety issue, or urgency, you may have to stop the job where you're, at and remind the employee of the safety issues or concern you have.

Addressing the employee should be done in privacy, if you are a large piece of property or even a business, and easy way is to ask the employee to take a walk with you as you wanted to speak to them about something, and showing something in the yard. And while you are walking you can discuss the concern you have with them, and they have their privacy. No employee, especially if you're planning on keeping them with you? Likes to be reprimanded or even discussed about policies in front of others unless, it is a emergency, then and only then should a discussion be on the policies at that time around others.


TIP:

In most cases the employer or manager is wanting to retain employment of the employee, therefore using respect, and some degree of caring when speaking to them will ensure the relationship you have with that employee, stays intact. Gone are the days of yelling at an employee and threatening to fire them, this was never a good idea and it rings true today.

**NOTE:**

There may be laws in place in your state or local jurisdiction that will pertain to the conduct and procedures needed for employees when discussing policy issues and concerns. Especially if the employee may be terminated at some point based on these meetings with an employee. States vary on employees' rights and how you conduct yourself on the enforcement of your policies with your employees, this knowledge will ensure you can avoid problems in the future if the employee needs to be terminated. Especially when it comes to collecting unemployment benefits, as many employees will state they were mistreated, or not properly informed, this is why when you review policy verbally, it is also good idea to have the employee sign a copy of the policy they violated. As simple initial and date is good enough, it also shows you're keeping records on the policy problems. It will be crucial to have policies set in place, so if needed, the managers in charge, or the owner will have the proper tools to address any policy or terminations.


**Mutual understanding:**

The breakdown of communication within the work environment is generally caused by two aspects. One, being poor management styles, and two being poor training.

Generally speaking most employee situations and difficulties can be avoided, if due diligence is observed in the beginning of your employees business relationship. Oftentimes a person can own a business, and operate that business very efficiently. They may know the duties that surround the physical work and mental work needed. They have become very efficient, and work hard to become a successful company. But this same company may have a high turnover of employees, and a difficult time with employee interactions. This is a great concern, as oftentimes, a troubled employee will spread these problems to other employees. These employees issues will be observed by coworkers, and several aspects of the business can possibly be harmed in that business. If you have a employee that is causing the company to not work as efficient as it has, this needs to be addressed at once. The longer your concerns over employee are allowed to fester, the more the possible extent of damage to your company could occur.

**Managing employees continued: Mutual Understanding, Reasoning .**

One cannot stress enough that running a company with employees, must have a very solid base to work from. Oftentimes difficult employees can also be blamed on the management styles or the ownership of the company. There are teachers that owned companies and manage them, then there are those that want everyone to know how good they are at managing, but are terrible teachers. When you have an employee, you want them to grow with the company, and if they have no prior knowledge of the services you are providing, it will become crucial that your training technique, is both efficient, and have a clear understanding of the limitations of a novice employee. We all learn how to do things, the perspective we have on something new, is the same perspective a novice employee will have. After all none of us simply bought a car got the keys and started driving. We had to take time learn the rules of the road, learn safety, as well as how to respect other drivers on the road. And how to operate within the law. This technique is not unlike learning how to drive a car. One must take clear and concise understanding, and a calm attitude towards those who are not as experienced as the managers, or trainers in the company.

There is a saying, there are no bad employees. But simply bad owners and managers. Some may scoff at that statement, but it is ultimately your training, ,your policies, and conduct that will guide anyone you hire. It will even control how you interact with clients. After all it is 100% the management team's responsibility to ensure employees that can meet the required standards, are employed at your company.

The fact that you hired a lazy, late, an unorganized employee is not the employees fault, it is the managements teams fault, or the people that screened him or her when they hired them. Let's think about this for a moment, you're a company and you Supply Services to the community, potential clients are most likely screening you, even before a service call or estimate. They may ask their neighbors, look you up to see if you have a license, maybe even ask family members and friends if they have had any interactions with your company? Even your customers will do due diligence before hiring you. If a customer hires you and is not happy with the work he/she did, but never researched a company or ask any questions, it would be on the customers not the service provider for that result. I know it sounds unfair but customers recourse unless there was negligence done is to simply not hire you again, if they're not happy with the service.(Not happy does not mean did not complete the job). As it is with your employee they may not do the job you like, so you have the opportunity of letting them go early on, if you do not see the potential you need. Also doing proper research on your employee prior to hiring them may save you a lot of heartache later on. I've seen some companies simply hire bodies to dig ditches or mow lawns, they see this as an employee only, and they're not willing to invest a lot of time, because their view is that they are doing a mundane job. This technique will almost definitely fail to provide adequate services for your company. Why is that? Because if you had not done proper research on your employee, and were hiring them simply to do a specific task, but are not willing to do any research on them because of that? You are ignoring a major role of company operations, that being your employees represent your company, how they dress, how they act, how they perform their jobs, and respect the job that they're doing ,will reflect directly on your ability to manager employees. This is not only seen by the public, it is seen by your other employees who may or may not show equal respect to these employees, since you did not take the hiring them seriously.

Managing employees conclusion:

The best rule of thumb is to hire an employee not just for current work needed, but you should be looking at the future potential of an employee. Keep in mind you may start out your business simply mowing lawns, and maybe then you a hire and employee to work with you full time mowing lawns? It is at that time that you hire the first employee for your business, well that is when you should be looking at the employees future potential. You may end up having this original employee become a job boss, or may even seek to have them doing estimates and helping to manage your company in the future? Doing your due diligence at the beginning, will save a lot of heartache. Why everybody needs a second chance, keep in mind to do background checks on any employees that you hire. This is not to prevent those who have paid their dues in the legal system from finding work. But you must protect the interests of your clients as well as the interest of your work environment.

Every aspect of your company from creating fliers, designing billing for a client's, and providing accurate estimates as well as hiring employees, all should be done with the same quality and precision.

I owned our company, and we had some very hardworking employees as well as some great customers. Many times our employees would spend hours doing some tedious jobs for our clients, such as pulling weeds. Pulling weeds has to be the least glamorous job in any of the landscape and lawn care businesses. It is also one of the most noticeable jobs by a customer. Keep this in mind you may spend 1 hour at a client's job, mowing lawns, trimming bushes, and even pulling weeds. And when you leave, if you have left just one small weed in the lawn or in the dirt, the client will notice the one small weed you left in the yard. It sounds picky, but imagine this as a scenario, you take your car to be painted and want it painted inside and out, so all the metal is the same color. But in the very back of the car, there is a one small 1/2 inch spot that was not painted. Upon arriving to pick up your vehicle and inspecting it you may notice the great quality of work that was done, until you arrive at the back of the car and notice that 1/2 inch square that was not painted. All of a sudden all the hard work that was done on your vehicle is erased in the customer's mind, as they now see only the service that was not completed.

You should have this great care in mind when you hire employees, your reflection and duty to your company will only be reflected in the employees that you hire. A customer will see you taking the job as serious as you want them to take it, and will notice where you cut corners.

This can be done by being clear during any job interviews prior to hiring, that the quality of work you are looking for, and the seriousness of the duties they perform, even down to pulling the weeds in the yard. It is that attention to detail that you must see for yourself, so you can relay this information and quality you want to your customers, as well as your employees. The results will be a structure within your company, that is both professional, and desired by the general public when looking for the services you provide. Of course no one is perfect, and even with all the due diligence you may end up with a employee that will not improve themselves, or meet the criteria you are looking for. If this occurs how quickly you address these issues and how you resolve them, will help guide you in future concerns, plus it will show coworkers and partners in your company that you take all operations seriously.

# Chapter 10: The winter games:

The key to a successful business is to have services available to your customers year round, however depending on where you are located available services at particular seasons will vary. Obviously if you live in Southern California, Arizona or New Mexico, you will not be shoveling snow or require a snow blower. The same can be said if you live in Alaska you may not be doing lawn care year round.

Part of this chapter is to give you alternative options to give your clients. It is important to not be a seasonal only business. During off seasons depending on where you live the ability to sustain a net income for yourself and your employees become more difficult. But it's not impossible, if you are aware of duties you can perform in your area.

The first thing you must consider is including these off services into your clients contracts,( we will go into additions during normal operations in a later chapter) and having seasonal duties included in your contract, will ensure that your clients continue to have you working on their property, even in the off seasons!

Winter, for the majority of the lower states, winter starts beginning of December and ends some were around March. This will vary depending if you are in the northwest, southwest or on the East Coast. However there are duties that are in common with those months. Here are some examples.

1. Pest control and insect prevention for lawns and plants.
2. Fall cleanups which can involve the removal of debris and leaves.
3. Ice prevention and snow removal.
4. Winterizing sprinkler systems which includes drainage.
5. Install drainage systems.
6. Flood prevention
7. Weed control during winter.
8. Moss & Mold control and prevention.
9. Pruning, on dormant plants and trees.
10. Pressure washing, for mold and moss removal
11. Gutter cleaning

These are just a few of the items that you can do during an off-season, of course the availability of these duties will depend your location. There will be some areas of the country where there will be down time, however looking at other areas you may be able to expand, to help your business stay afloat. There are many plants that need caring for during the winter months. If you look at the list provided there'll be times of the year, that a proper times for these. Looking at the list at least half, if not more should be able to be implemented in the majority of the United States.

**The winter games continued:**

Looking at the 10 most common services you can provide in off seasons, we will explain these starting with number one.

**Pest control and prevention**, this can also include mold control as well as pest control. This is done usually late fall to early spring. But will vary with climate changes, that can and do vary each year.

Pest control itself can include prevention of lawn grubs, mites and prevention on several plants including roses and many flowered plants. The application of pest control may vary within your jurisdiction too. You will have to contact your local offices that oversee pest control to know whether not you will need a special license to apply chemicals. Generally speaking lawn and plants are within acceptable lawn care boundaries in most states. However structural pest control in most areas does require a specialized license. So check, and avoid getting fined.

**Fall cleanups,** can be carried out from October to January, depending on the services you're providing. During the off-season and depending on the weather you have, in your may include bad weather debris that can be created during the fall and thru to spring. This can include extra debris in the yards as well as leaf cleanups. Cleanups can involve hauling away debris, or simply moving it to the curb. This will vary depending on what is acceptable in the area you live. But generally speaking, if your client has many trees ( that are not evergreen) you will have a certain amount of debris and leaves to clean up. How you choose to supply the service and cost of services will be up to you, but there are two options. One, is to include this in your services for your client. That means each week you can come out spend a an allotted amount of time, and begin the debris removal. Or you may opt to offer this service to your clients as an additional charge in a seasonal flier. It is advised if you are wanting to keep a year round service, to include these services with your contract for debris removal. Your clients will see that they're not paying extra for that service but meanwhile you are providing it.

**Ice prevention and snow removal**. Many companies in the northern states operate snow removal services within parking lots, and homes during the off-season. This can be a fulltime job and often justifies the purchase of snow removal equipment. Most major cities have a snow removal service, that are only used on public access streets, and not parking lots. Companies need to have their parking lots clear, so their customers can to continue to use their services. This is why it's important to provide these services if the ability is in your area. In a residential service, having snow removal may be the difference of your client getting to work, or staying home that day. Providing this type of service can be invaluable! It should also be noted even if you do not have snow in the area you live, during the winter months many states have a ice. Using the proper products such as salt to remove the ice, or to apply for prevention, can keep your clients safe, and help ensure there's no disruption in the services you have during off seasons.

**Winterizing sprinkler systems** which includes drainage. Something to note is approximately 80% of the United States has areas that can drop down below freezing at certain times of the year. Also during the wet seasons, proper drainage should be in place. Oftentimes a person is not aware of where the drainage is needed, especially in new homes or areas that have been neglected.

**Draining the sprinkler system** is crucial to avoid breaking pipes. In fact it would only take one or two days at 1.1 degrees C' or 30 degrees F, for pipes to freeze and up to where they would break. There's a misconception that water pipes underground will not freeze. They will! In many areas pipes are buried from 4 to 7 inches depending on where you live, this is more than enough exposure to have pipes freeze. Moreover the amount of damage caused by freezing pipes each year, tallies into the millions in this country. However most damages could be avoided by simply draining the systems prior to the temperature changes. This is a simple and cost effective way to ensure the pipes stay ready for the next year. Plus tools to drain the pipes, generally only costs a few $100 depending on the pipe size and the area covered. Generally landscape contractors that have commercial properties will install a drainage adapter making it much easier to drain a system when needed. That is why keeping these two aspects of your potential services in mind can help your finances. Plus this can definitely be a plus to inform your customers, that not only are you saving them money, but you may save them hardship, if they have water flooding their yards or property due to a pipe break. It is important to note that backflow systems themselves can have enough water to crack, and that is why it is crucial to have the entire system drained of water to avoid any systems failing. It is important to note that draining the sprinkler system is also something you can add into your contract with your current customers. This will ensure again more services you can provide in the off months. It is also something you can put in your fliers when sending your billing.

**Flood prevention**, this is usually reserved for landscape companies, as it will involve changing the land itself in many cases. Like drainage mentioned above, you may find out there's an issue with your drainage as well as a possible cause to a flooding issue. This would require someone to act quickly and have the knowledge to work on the property in adverse conditions and harsh weather. Depending on the weather you have during the winter months you may have issues such as flash floods or melting snow, that can cause an awful lot of issues with flooding. So it is crucial that only a professional attempt these duties, obviously this would not be something normally put into a maintenance contract, because issues cannot be foreseen.

**Moss & mold plus, weed control**. We have put these two topics together as oftentimes these services can go hand in hand. Having these services placed into a contract will provide security for your jobs during winter months. Plants will begin to have molded issues when there are a combination of warm and cool days. You may notice in some areas of the country in early fall the sidewalks will appear to turn black in areas. This is a sign that mold is growing and the weather has become temperate enough for it to flourish. This also means that your lawns and plants need to be cared for and looked after for moss and mold. A good way of seeing the potential for these conditions is watching the humidity. rise and fall.

Generally speaking when temperatures above 40°and less than 60 degrees, with a ratio of humidity of over 70% sets the conditions for mold to exist as well as moss. Now these conditions can vary, but this is an ideal situation for them to grow. Depending on where you live , and frequencies of these variations, can depend on how quickly these conditions develop.

Weed control is something that should be done in all open grounding areas as well as rock and bark, you may not think the winter months are great time to do weed control, but it is. Many times the wet weather can effect residual of previously applied chemicals. Depending on where you live and the chemicals allowed during the seasons. There should be a slow acting weed control product you can use in your area. Casoron(tm)(c) as well as granulated salt are both products that are used as weed control. Your local availability of products will vary, and maybe also guided by certain regulations. Please be sure before applying products, that they can be applied to the ground area in need of prevention. These services are something that can be added to the contracts and help preserve future services.

**Pruning,** generally speaking the ideal time to do pruning is when the plant is not germinating, has gone dormant, or is no longer seeping sap. Pruning is not simply chopping off limbs, and making things look presentable. Many plants require training, to stay healthy and to provide the fruits and seeds they create. However a plant can be harmed greatly by not being pruned it the right time o year or in the correct way. We cannot include how this should be done to specific plants, given the criteria for the book does not allow me to include it. However we will be looking at how two books for the landscape and Gardner in the future look for **us** an Amazon(yes that was plug).

**Pressure washing,** like snow removal, pressure washing is something that can be done when the seasons change. Generally speaking customers will call for pressure washing begin in early fall and continue well into spring depending on the growth of moss or mold in the area. It should be noted that a majority of the state's do require specific licensing to use a pressure washer, and can vary depending on the intended application. We're adding this as an option due to the fact many landscapers and lawn care professionals are using pressure washing, as a addition to their off season services they provide. Pressure washing is using high pressure water lines usually by a gas powered unit that allows a person to clean moss and mold off of several different types of surfaces. And this is where the variation on licensing may be applicable in your area, please check first.

**Winter games final conclusion.**  Gutter cleaning, this is an easy service that can be applied easily to your services, based on the fact that most lawn care and landscapers in the scope of their business use the same materials and equipment during the year that can be used for gutter cleaning. Making it an ideal migration into the off-season. It can be included with some of the additional services at that time. Think about adding gutter cleaning into year contracts with customers, as this is something you only do maybe possibly twice at the most per year. But is something that no client likes to do themselves, and by including this type of service, you'll almost guarantee they will allow that to be put in their contract for an added extra charge.

Having off seasons does not mean you need to stop working. It means you need to think, what do my customer want?. Yea round customers have duties that they do not want to perform themselves, but may often do it themselves, because they're unsure who to trust or who to call. If you already have a good relationship with your current customer? They will also most likely want to have services is added by your company. It is important to make sure customers aware that they can have a contract, with no added cost when these other services need to be completed. Its a win, win situation !

Adding such services as these to a contract in the beginning will allow you to work possibly year round without any interruptions. It also allows you to include these services as optional add-on throughout the year. Perhaps in late summer early fall within your billing cycle you can add the option to purchase? However you choose to pass out fliers or include them within the newsletter communicating this information is crucial for stability. You could include it as a special addition , something that's along the lines of a fall special gutter cleaning, and cleanups, or have your sprinkler system flushed by a professional. Let us take care of all your mold, moss, and weed problems year round? Of course you'll come up with your own way of advertising this to your customers.

Winter services, may not have to be referred to as downtime services, or off-season, in fact if you run your business correctly these additions will become part of your entire business structure, meaning that you'll never have a down day throughout the year.

Again this varies allot on how you run your business, and how many services you want to try in include. This is not something anyone writing a book such as myself can advise you on. Even though I have done this for decades it's not something a person can advise you on doing. To take those steps will require your comfort level on adding them. It is advised one does not simply add all of the above in their first year of operations, unless they have prior experience.

In closing this chapter, keep in mind that winter services can attract a lot of business. During our operations we had winter months that were quite cold, and summer months that were quite hot. But seldom were we without work, simply because we were diverse, by offering services that would help our clients year round.

# Chapter 11: Problem solving:

In this chapter I will be covering some basic techniques to resolve issues in your business. Up to this point this book has covered a variety of topics. The goal will be in this chapter to give you a step by step process of problem solving. You may have up to this point develop some skills depending on your work background, and ability to work with others. This may be a plus when resolving problems. However it is very important to realize, that working for a company, is very much different then owning a company, when it comes to problem solving. In fact there a lot of things to consider from this perspective. So I will break it down into several sections.

**Step one,** develop a view from all sides. You may be aware of your policies and your work ethics as well as contracts, however when  problem solving one has to look at all sides of an issue that helped develop it. This means you must step aside for a moment, and look at it "only" from a customer's point of view as an example. Then you must look at it from your "employees" point if you "only" as another example. Then you must step aside and look at the financial affects that has brought you to this point, and how the outcome will change the course of your business.

**Step two,** remove the blame game. If you go into a problem solving with the self righteous decision mind set, that mean you're correct and everybody is wrong. Well you now have ended a discussion in problem solving, before it started. You may be coming to the discussion because there is a violation of your contract or policies, and that may make you feel you are in the right. This may also encourage you to push that opinion on others involved. This would be a huge mistake as you already know what you feel has driven you problem solve. So taking this mindset in pushing it on others will immediately come across as an aggressive stance. If you are trying to resolve the issue with a customer over a contract this can end discussions, before they began. Keep in mind you are not in the place of problem solving if you'll only wanting to know who's right and tell others who are wrong. Yes it can be difficult, but you must take your time, even take a few moments to yourself to breathe, before you engage in problem solving.

**Step three,** financial liability. This means what is effected in the discussions, and at what cost are the problems being solved. You may work extremely hard to resolve it as soon as possible. However one must also look at how it financially effects the company. At this particular point, it is not really relevant how a problem with financial ability your customer has, as they can either pay for the services to resolve the issue, or they cannot. But it needs to be something to consider on your end. Customers will either pay for something or they won't. But you have to look at the financial impact on your company and employees, as well as materials. But this is taking to all the above information on steps one in two, into consideration, and now it's time to decide and act. But is important to know is your decisions economically sound?.

**Problem solving, step three continued**


**Scheduling,** this can be tricky, depending on the situation you're in. You may need to resolve an issue at a particular job site, however you are booked for all your time and availability. But you must solve the problem that has come up on the job site, of the current an existing customer. As an example you may have a broken sprinkler system on a current customer that has a yearlong contract with you, you also have a new sprinkler system that's being installed the same day on the other side of town. How do you problem solve this? Imagine it's in the middle of summer and your customer has a new lawn you just installed a month ago, but now the sprinkler system needs repair? There's simply not enough time in the day to do every job in a 24 hour time frame. So one must look at scheduling and rearranging projects to solve the problem. You don't want to lose the new customer you have with a big project, That is a great job with a full sprinkler system being installed, you also do not want to damage the new lawn you just installed, or your lose the current longstanding customer you have. That is why using the steps that are included as a process to help you filter out how to resolve things. There is an answer within these solutions on problem solving. And it will take you having discussions to understand the overview of what needs doing.


**Step four, the resolution.** At this point you've come to a conclusion and verified that your final decision that will resolve the issues. You will find it using some of these tools to help you resolve future issues. It is important to note that a resolution should not contain special treatment to be resolved. NOTE THIS: If you make special treatment arrangements with a current customer or employee. You're setting the standard that other employees or customers may seek in the future as their own personal resolution. Case in point, Joe your employee for three years has not shown up on time today. You find out he stayed up late last night before and now overslept. You wave any problems with Joe because he's been there long time. Then the same situation happens with another employee and you now created a situation that may set precedents for other employees be treated the same way Joe was. Another example is you have a route for your services, the longtime customer ask you if you can do their services on Friday because they really want to be in great condition for the weekend each time.

They been with you a longtime so you decide to do it. But.... Then their neighbor calls up seeing that you're out there and also wants to have it done on that day. You're making a special adjustment for the longtime customer now you put yourself in the situation of having to spend more time in a particular area that you may not have. This may work in some cases but not others, so it is important to look down the line and see what may occur, and how you going to resolve it. It's not just looking at the resolution in front of you, is also looking at the decision you make today, and how they're going to effect your company, your employees, and customers later.

### Troubleshooting and scheduling.

One of the toughest parts of the business whether you are a landscaper or lawn care professional is scheduling and troubleshooting issues while on the job. Most people when they own a business have visions of booking services for months at a time, and working all the time making money to equal a great income. In the ideal situation, you would have in just one day, a neighborhood of 50 customers all living right next to each other. You could simply push your lawnmower to the next house and easily knock out 50 customers. However it's never as simple as that. While there are companies that can try, when doing landscaping that will secure a housing track during the construction phase, and will continue that maintenance for years to come. These are not commonplace for the majority of businesses. The majority of these type of services are very similar to those in most Home Services Industries, in fact the housekeeping business is very similar in the type of technique used.

So how do you schedule for clients you do not even have yet? And should you dedicate certain days for maintenance and days for one Time Services?

**Let's look at the first question how you schedule for clients who haven't had yet?** The best way is to first go to your local county office or retail store and purchase a map of the service area. Some map books used in the trucking industry are small enough to keep in your vehicle. What you'll want to do (depending on the size of the city, and the area you plan on working in) Is the section the area's out by days of the week, an easier way to do this is starting off Monday A. Tuesday B., And so on. On your map you will want to use a highlighting marker to draw out a border of the areas you wish to cover. Ideally you should begin your business under a section A:, the section you have marked out. It is easier to start of the beginning of the week with your business to allow the ending of the week to do estimates in planning for future jobs. Now I'm sure some people may not agree with this idea, they may think it's better to start at the end of the week and work your way toward Monday, leaving Friday's as the key maintenance jobs for your customers. Why this may sound like a good idea you will eventually run out of room at the end of the week not the beginning. And being most work weeks start on Monday, it will make it more organized for you to do that. You will have E: area, that would represent a Friday on the maps. Regardless of where you live, you know there are properties on either side of town that have a higher income bracket that you may want to set for the end of the week on your maintenance schedules. The reason being the majority of people that have a higher income expect to have a clean , ,neat property and are much more picky about how it looks going into a weekend. This is not saying neglect other customers by having them on Mondays, as it will be your responsibility to make sure the properties are maintained well enough on a Monday that they will be good enough until you come back the next week. Do not cut corners! But there are things you can do on property to make them seem more appealing.

**Troubleshooting and scheduling continued:**

Going back to the original promise of sectioning off the areas for maintenance, will allow you the ability to have open time throughout the week. You may start on Monday, and schedule your business and only have five or six jobs that day. If you have passed out fliers in your Monday schedule area you may be called even that evening for an estimate. Something I have done on days when we were starting out was to do a new clients property, and then pass out fliers on that block. Looking at our chapter on fliers you'll see how you can design flyers for a particular area. May even want to let people know in your fliers you are now new in the area and doing their neighbor's property. And then you can point it out to them when you do an estimate. So keep this in mind when sectioning off areas to the to leave time open on each day.

Now I know, what do you do when you  have completely filled up an entire Monday through Friday schedule? This is why having sections marked off will allow you to customize those areas as needed. Say for example you are only doing services by yourself with no additional employee, once you need another employee to help take off the slack. well this is when you can increase the amount of work you can do in a given day. If you have one or two employees with you, and that maxed out the amount of people you can take with you one each job, this only the time to evaluate whether or not having any additional trucks or routes are needed. This is also a time when you can use the additional employee to begin a separate route. The best way to do that is to mark off a Monday and split the schedule for Monday into two sections instead of one. As this will allow you or the extra crew, and truck to be in the general area. This way it allows you to keeping full control of the access, and duties needed on each property. Some people will take a new vehicle and truck and send them off to other areas. This is where I've seen the errors made, as a business owner it is important that you can manage the properties. And if you are very new at this you'll want to be in the close proximity of your jobs when you cannot be there. Placing and your route in the hands of others, across town or in other cities makes it difficult to manage. It also makes it difficult, if you must leave your current job and go see what's up and another job. Imagine your second employee is out mowing lawns, and knocks off the top of the sprinkler head breaking a pipe in the process. He has not been trained on the replacement or how to fix the pipe, and of gives you a call. If you are in another town, this means dropping what you're doing and heading off to the job putting your schedule and routes out of order. This is why any additions to your business should be considered that their completions are done in close proximity of your location that day.

To grow out into other areas or cities it will be important that you're experienced employees are left with the longest and most important route days. As your company grows obviously one cannot be in every city or scheduled area at once. At this particular point, as your business grows beyond its current ability, only then will you have to consider a separate manager. As was discussed in previous chapters if you have a partner in the business this will allow you to customize the daily maintenance into those areas. It would be very smart if there were two partners to split up a Monday schedule and allow it to grow. As the business grows one partner could then take on in other area on the same day and so on. Once you reach for maximum growth and will be adding an additional crew that is not involved in the management or ownership, then you are ready to take the next step.

# Tips and tricks of the trade.

We hope you found this book helpful and informative the next several pages of our book will includes tips and how to's, of the landscape and lawn maintenance trade.

The top 50 mistakes a new landscape and lawn care business makes.

1. Expanding their business too quickly.
2. Spending too much on equipment before balancing sufficient income.
3. Not taking proper time to hire the right employees for the job.
4. Not communicating properly to their clients. Lack of details on the contract.
5. Blaming others for the downfall, or loss of business.
6. Not reinvesting profits into business.
7. Not getting proper licensing when it is required.
8. Arguing on the job, a great way to show others how unprofessional you are.
9. Advertising beyond their ability to justify costs.
10. Bringing personal and Home Life to the job. Work is work, leave home at home.
11. Do not take personal calls from your family or friends unless it's an emergency.
12. Dressing professionally, being dirty is one thing looking unprofessional is another.
13. Keeping the equipment and vehicles clean.
14. Not standing behind services provided.
15. Not keeping proper tax records, and payroll information.
16. Spending too much on an advertising for wrong services.
17. Not using social media and web sites to advance the business.
18. Not putting in writing, contract changes.
19. Not getting proper deposits on large jobs.
20. Using e-mail or text, instead of solving problems in person.
21. Not including in contracts, hauling and debris removal cost.
22. Not adding delivery costs and material handling.
23. Not including General Services in the contract, to lowball the estimate.
24. Not being respectful, of competitors in the area, or a customers past service provider.
25. Bad mouthing past employees or competitors, to others.
26. Not paying vendors on time, or being inconsiderate of delivery dates and time.
27. Not giving employees proper breaks, you must insist that employees take breaks.
28. Not including a noncompetitive clause when hiring employees.
29. Paying an employee under the table, should never be done it is unsafe and unprofessional.
30. Not being courteous to other drivers when traveling to and from job sites.

31. Not providing adequate hydration on job sites.  Or making local bathroom breaks availabilities.
32. Not securing a business checking account.
33. Not registering their business, or in some cases Trade marking and copyrighting their material.
34. Not cleaning equipment when finished, should be done each day.
35. Not taking time to maintain vehicles, you vehicle or equipment failure is the number one thing that interrupts a job.
36. Pruning, fertilizing, the wrong times of year.
37. Not practicing proper safety, hearing and eye protection, as well as gloves are a must.
38. Not doing a walkthrough at the completion of each and every job you do.
39. Not securing gates, many have lost customers by leaving a gates open, and I allowing a customers pets to escape.
40. Locking keys in the vehicle, so keep a spare somewhere you can get to.  It happens more than you think.
41. Doing jobs that are not within their licensing, this could cost you your business and possibly carry heavy fines.
42. Not being considerate of neighboring properties,(blowing debris, early noise,)
43. Taking on weekend jobs, while tempting family comes first, on occasion is acceptable.  Remember why you're working.
44. Not returning phone calls promptly too concerned customers.
45. Do not give customers your cell phone number, have an office phone at home this is the best way.
46. Be on time, it is better to be at half an hour early to a job than 1/2 hour late, yes people do notice.
47. Speaking professionally to clients, but not talking down to them.  Obviously you have some knowledge in the job you are doing that there is no reason to make a customer feel stupid.
48. Not being polite at all times.
49. Not leaving a card, or invoice and leaving a job.  Very important to let your client know when you were there.
50. Not documenting, or taking pictures of before and after jobs.  This is a good idea for many reasons.  With today's smart phones it takes 2 seconds to save your job info from today.

**The top hidden in secrets that can make your business run more smoothly. Over the years while in business we actually created some of the easier ideas, as well as will be including other top secrets.**

Tarps, you may see debris going down the roadway in a truck and it's covered by a tarp? The great news it is there are many uses or a tarp.

- Lay a tarp on the bottom of the truck and loading leaves and debris onto it. When you arrive at your dumping station, you can simply pull the tarp out and take 90% of the debris with you. Why this may not work with lumber it works great for grass and leaves as well as lightweight material. We found a tarp could last a month or more and saved us time.
- It's perfect for moving debris from one place to another. You can lay down and load the debris onto it. Then you and a helper can drag carry the material to the truck.
- It can be used for leafed cleanups, by laying down the tarp and raking the material onto it.
- You can also use a riding tractor or mower to pull the tarp and use it as a skid that is flexible. Depending on the terrain if it's soft enough you could use a tarp and pull quite a distance for us, this was ideal for leaves and other lightweight debris gathered at long distances.

The weedeater, you may or may not be aware there's been big changes in the way of weedeater is used in the job. They all have transverse carburetors, meaning they can be turned to nearly any angle and will continue to run. This makes these an excellent choice for edging of lawns. It should be noted extreme care should be used when using it weedeater for edging lawns, as debris can travel quite a distance it is not uncommon to hit a car with a rock or something like that if you're not careful. The weedeater also comes nowadays with several attachments some of the major commercial brands have hedging adapters, blades and many other attachments. It is highly advised ( if you can afford) if you can afford higher-end machine to use, as with the attachments can allow you to carry less equipment.

When over-seeding a lawn, or installing sod, they make a machine called a sod cutter. Now normally a sod cutter is used only in the manufacturing of sod. However many rental companies carry this equipment. What this means is you will not be rototilling a area, you can actually cut the old lawn right out of the yard itself, it also creates rolls of lawn pieces, making it very easy to dispose of or use for landfill. These generally cut down a depth about 2 to 4 inches, and leaving a great area to add topsoil and either seed or add sod. We have used this on many of our jobs, and found it to result in a very clean looking service, and cut our time to complete by over half.

Compressors, normally you see this in a shop of some kind, or you use it to fill the tires on your car and your equipment. But having a portable compressor is also helpful for clearing out clogs in sprinkler heads and lines themselves. They do make 12volt compressors or you may be able to hook one up to your truck itself using the belt system in the truck engine compartment. This allows you to perform any duty needing an air source, and would only carry hose with you instead of having to carry a major compressor. Most people do not realize that a lot of the newer equipment especially commercial equipment has inflatable tires, this is also helpful for cleaning equipment.

More hidden tips.

Did you know, you can get soil for free? If you have a large enough area you can use the debris such as grass and leaves that you get from job sites and create your own compost on your property. While this is generally only something a large landscape company can do. Recycling the debris saves on fees that you may have to pay at the dumps, it also saves on trips there as well. And it allows you to have soil to take with you on the jobs absolutely free. Large composters to run around $500 to $1000, but may be worth it the long run. ( if you had the area to work with). Also saving plants that are reusable. In our landscaping business we often removed many plants that customers simply did not want, but the plants were in good condition themselves. So we would take them back and re-pot them and then have extra plants that we could provide to our customers that may want them at a very discounted price.

Recycling, as of the time of this book, laws changed making plastics and the like non-recyclable, it is important that you take great care in the debris that you develop and how you are disposing of it. Garbage cans are a great resource to use as opposed to plastic bags. Now I know you're thinking everyone will probably use a garbage can. But carrying around 10 garbage cans is more difficult carrying plastic bags and many landscape companies and lawn care maintenance do this. And that debris left over from those bags ends up in the landfill. So it is worth your time and money to invest when you can into garbage cans, or as noted earlier use tarps anything you can do to cut down on the amount of debris are putting in the landfill. n( you can also use old used tarps folded over for weeds blocks.

Snow shovels, they can be used for more than just snow. We found during the fall and winter when we needed to clean debris from road gutters it worked awesome. Also a heavy snow shovel can work as a large dustpan when used with a push broom allows more debris to be picked up in a short amount of time. And they are aluminum and light.

Riding lawnmowers versus riding tractors, if you are strictly doing lawns and never any other type of service, a riding mower may be ideal for large properties. But don't not purchase inexpensive versions and riding tractors. With the advancements in today's machinery, there are many attachments for today's riding mowers. They can pull behind brush hogs, small trailers to haul rock side etc.. Furthermore riding tractors tend to have a lower torque ratio which means they can pull more weight and carry more weight. Depending on the models you purchase they can run anywhere from several hundred dollars to several thousand dollars. As noted earlier chapters only purchase what you will need, you may want to buy the best and the biggest but may not be practical based on your current conditions.

Blowers, generally these are used to clear dust and leaves from an area often cleaning up after a service call. However Blowers can be used for many other things. They can be used to clean out the gutters on homes. You would have to secure yourself safely to do so, but they make clearing out gutters easy. But always observed extreme safety, and be sure you are insured to do so. A blower can also be used in conjunction with other people using a blower. In forming a sort of wall you can walk side-by-side together and clear off leaves in large areas. In effect tripling the amount of force you have, it is amazing how quickly three people working together with Blowers can clean up an area.

Push mowers, now generally speaking a person picks out a push mower to fit their size height and job requirements. But just a quick tip always purchase a push mower that has a side discharge. And rear self-propelled, but the point is having a side discharge opens the possibilities of using the mower for more than simply mowing a lawn. Mulching can be used, but is only ideal for certain situations as it can lead to thatch build up and clogs in mowers.

More Tips

And here a couple of tips for around the house and shop that you can take with you to use on your jobs.

- Motor oil can be poured into a small mustard squirt bottle and used to lubricate and clean your equipment at half the price of what spray lubricants cost.
- Keep a sharper for knives and pruners on the vehicle this will guarantee you have sharp equipment.
- Buy a couple of very inexpensive gloves and keep them in the vehicle as spares. I cannot tell you how many times we lost our gloves or misplace them and were able to use the spares we kept with us.
- Always have enough hearing protection and eye protection for everyone will be on the job.

This will conclude the tips section and our ideas that work, you may come up with your own ideas that will work. Please keep in mind this book created with decade's worth of work in mind, so we found the easiest and most cost effective ways to do things, yet still provide a great quality of service our customers and ourselves could be proud of.

IMPORTANT!
Notes: please use the above tips with caution, and knowledge of the equipment that you use. Using equipment in a different manner than is intended, could cause harm or damage You can gauge whether something is a good idea or not based on these couple of things, is it safe for you and your employees, is it safe for the general public and your customers, and is it harmful to your equipment or

other objects may be in the surrounding areas. So please use with caution any tips that you have seen to this point.

# Chapter 13:
# List of equipment for lawn maintenance and landscape maintenance.

This is not a comprehensive list but a general knowledge list of items you will want to keep on your truck and with you when on the job. Your list may vary. And may depend on the size of your truck and maintenance.

- Lawnmower and a spare if applicable.
- Weed eater, extra line and repair tool for this equipment.
- A blower, preferred version is a backpack blower for larger areas and to avoid fatigue.
- Rakes and shovels, even if not needed on specific jobs are handy to have.
- Push brooms, and a dustpan.
- Pruners, for large and for small branches as well as hand pruners for roses and alike.
- Safety glasses, and spares.
- Hearing protection, for all people that will be on the job.
- Gas containers, and two-stroke oil if applicable.
- Bungee cords, and straps. You should include rope as well.
- Tarp, and garbage cans. Also tiedowns for the lids.
- Weed poppers, and small spade shovels.
- 5 gallon paint buckets. These are great for picking up small weeds around the property.
- Spare tools, you should examine your equipment and be sure that you have proper tools to fit the nuts bolts and screws for each item on the equipment.
- A water container were please to keep extra drinking water.
- A spare key located on the vehicle or trailer for the truck.
- A spare battery for your cell phone, should be kept in the vehicle along with a cigarette lighter charger.
- Orange safety cones, makes it easier for those to see you and may be required as well.
- Spare business cards, should be in your glove box at all times.
- Keep a binder or notebook to take the job notes for future reference.
- Camera if your phone does not have one.
- A spare tire for the truck and for the trailer.
- Spare contracts, I cannot tell you how many times a potential customer would walk down the street or stop and ask is to give them a bid on the

property. Being ready gives you the ability to possibly secure a job right down the street so carry these with you at all times.

- Extra spark plugs for the equipment you carry, as well as starting fluid.
- It is always a good idea to have at least a small copy can or container toolbox or what have you with extra bolts nuts etc.
- Maps of area jobs are in.
- First Aid Kit, and Fire Extinguisher.

It would be impossible to list all the equipment needed for a landscape company, as they include such things as sod cutters, trenchers, a backhoe and many other pieces of equipment depending on the size of your company. So why this book is designed to help landscape companies, covering all possible equipment would not be practical.
Doing the job, tips and hints you may not be aware of.

- Mowing. Did you know that aiming the outside right side of the mower with the direction of the discharge whether it's going into a bag or out the lawn is the best way to mow lawn? Facing the direction which is generally the right side of the mower standing behind it allows the debris to exit away from the direction you're going. This is especially helpful when the grass is wet keeping the discharge on the outside as you to complete a circle or an outward direction and not clog up your mowers as easily.

- Weed eating and edging. There are two ways to do this, you can edge the lawn prior to mowing if the grass is longer than 4 inches. However if you are mowing a standard height lawn at 2 to 3 inches it is best to edge the lawn afterwards so you can catch any areas the lawnmower did not hit. If you're using the weedeater around objects that may overlap the lawn then is a good time to mow after you have weedeated the lawn. This is something you get used is to let the lawnmower pick up the debris that the weedeater has created. However edging a lawn you can use the blower afterwards as well.

- Loading debris, depending on what you are hauling on the property, it can be backbreaking work. You've no doubt heard the expression work smarter not harder? The idea behind this is to make sure you are using the buddy system to carry heavy cans, or using a tarp to drag materials to the truck. The train your employees to make sure if they need help, to get help.


- Where to start on a property, this gets kind of interesting if you are a sole person mowing lawns by yourself. And you have a front and back lawn to mow you cannot obviously keep your equipment and truck within view while working. That is a concern when working alone as you may have valuables in the truck as well as equipment you cannot keep an eye on. Please keep this in mind when working by yourself to secure everything before going into a backyard for a extended period of time.

## Chapter 14: Some closing thoughts.

This book was written to try and help those looking to get into landscape and lawn care maintenance to learn from the successes we had as well as the hardships in learning how to run these businesses. My experience goes all the way back to the 1970s when me and my friends would push a lawnmower around the neighborhood mowing lawns fully weeds and even growing our own plants in the backyard at our house to sell your customers. We're little entrepreneurs indenting the know it, but that would set the mold for us running our own successful landscape business for decades.

Prior to me opening our business in 1995, I had worked for three separate major landscape companies. I also have studied business law, business management as well as consulting prior to opening my business in 1995. So the experience that I am bringing to this book is not just years of pushing a lawnmower and digging ditches, it's years of negotiating and maneuvering our business into the best possible scenario for success. Were there hardships and mistakes, you bet but we took great care to learn from those mistakes and hardships and to make our business stronger because of it. Everyone does things differently, but our business model proved to be the most successful landscape and maintenance company in our area for decades. We brought a new level of professionalism had not previously been seen in the industry. When computers were just coming about, we were the first company to have electronic billing and to have a website all this is the Internet was just becoming a small thing later to become much bigger. We knew the future was going to be and we will aim for it, and made our business very successful.

Will reading this book make you successful, absolutely not. This is not one of those self-help books were they lied to you and tell you all the secrets are contained within the small little pages. What this book will do is provide a solid basis for a very strong company to succeed. If you are willing to do what's needed to break a path to your success. I have put this in the back of the book as opposed to the front because if you read the book to this point and you understand exactly what I'm saying. Putting this in the front of the book gives a false pretense of what the book is about and people think that we will be solving all their problems in a book. That is basically impossible for anyone that promises you that consulting your business will lead to success is not telling the truth. But success is possible using the structure we used. We have gone on to other areas of our lives enclosed are landscape business, but it was very important to provide this information to other people. You may look upon the Internet and you will find very little information to anyone that wants to start a blue-collar business and as why we came about trying to design a book that was short simple to the point with some good solid bases and information that may help you get started. It also gives the existing company a chance to see weak spots that may be in their business they have not thought of before.

I am also providing this book at a very small cost of just under a dollar, you may ask yourselves why am I selling something so cheap with all these answers. No there's nothing else to buy, you will be billed later for something else, this is a honest attempt to provide needed information for companies need it. For far too long people see others struggling and want to profit after it. The small amount being charged for this book is to entice others to buy it and take a look at their business without thinking they just invested a lot of money. By making it cost-effective it allows the business to find this information without spending hundreds of dollars on consulting fees and buying books it basically tell you how to plant plants and mow lawns but not how to run a business. That's where this book comes in.

Within the pages of this book I placed common sense, giving the ability of the new entrepreneur confidence to strive be better. And for the existing entrepreneur to give an overview of their business model and compare to a model we have prepared here.

Being in this business is awesome, and depending where you live imagine each day stepping outside and enjoying the environment you live in. Some very nice things tend to happen when you're doing landscaping is you notice things around you probably never noticed before you worked or owns your business. You start noticing the sky being more blue, and you notice nature a lot more. In fact your whole nature becomes one with the outdoors. It became to the point where we could no how soon the rains would come this next year, if it would be a cold or snowing winter and how hot the summers would be all by watching what was happening outside. We were often way more accurate in our predictions of the weather than the newscasters were. That made it kind of find ourselves to know exactly was going to happen and when to happen which gave us an edge often in pursuing our business ventures. You'll find that you make many new friends within the business environment, from suppliers to vendors and the like you'll build relationships, possibly even form credit it needed all from supplying your customers with great service.

So why would we open a landscape business, and run it for over 20 years when we had legal backgrounds and professional education? We did so to show that anyone can run this business, and we wanted to share our professional attitude towards landscape in lawn care that we passed along to others. We did not know that at the time that we were going to be passing it along, but as our reputation grew more and more in the community saw that landscapers could be professional, look professional act professional. This set a standard that also made our customers feel good about having is that the property, being the first in the area to ever have uniforms it sure set a standard that is followed to this day. Many of the tricks and tips that you see in this book are designed by as and are now used in many areas of this country simply by word of mouth. Now we have pass this information along to you so you can have a successful business. Not only that in this book I am including a e-mail address that you can use task as questions about your new business. All included with purchasing this book.

Coming soon, look for our new additions to self-help business books.

The writer of this book Paul Cordell,  Is an a established business owner with over 25 years experience in the Landscape and Blue Collar industry. Having owned one of the largest Landscape businesses of its time. He has since retired and is providing you insight to the not so know world of running a lawn care, or landscape business.

Paul, has studied Business Law, Business Accounting as well as computer science and even worked as Counselor Supervisors for many years.  Paul has worked as a Service Industry Director and has helped protect many right of people and businesses in state legislation.

In this book you will find solution to:

- Starting a Business in Lawn Care or Landscaping.
- Taxes and Billing
- Trouble shooting and problem solving.
- Partnerships and employees.
- How to hire, and terminate positions.
- Buying equipment and leasing.
- How to work year round where ever you live.
- Tricks of the Trade...

And much more.......

www.ingramcontent.com/pod-product-compliance
Lightning Source LLC
Chambersburg PA
CBHW072016230526
45468CB00021B/1603